WHY DO I GET SUNBURN?

+ and other questions about skin +

Angela Royston

Heinemann Library
Chicago, Illinois

Designed by Joanna Sapwell and StoryBooks
Illustrations by Nick Hawken
Originated by Ambassador Litho
Printed by South China Printers, China

07 06
10 9 8 7 6 5 4

Library of Congress Cataloging-in-Publication Data
Royston, Angela
 Why do I get a sunburn? : and other questions about skin / Angela Royston.
      p. cm. -- (Body matters)
Includes index.
Summary: Answers common questions about human skin.
  ISBN 1-40340-203-5 (HC)   ISBN 1-40340-458-5 (PB)
  1. Skin--Juvenile literature. [1. Skin.] I. Title. II. Series.
  QP88.5 .R69 2002
  612.7'9--dc21

                              2002003544

Acknowledgments
The author and publishers are grateful to the following for permission to reproduce copyright material:
pp. 4, 13 Stone; p. 5 Corbis; p. 6, 10, 21 Science Photo Library; pp. 8, 9, 20, 22, 24, 25, 28 Gareth Boden; pp. 11, 17, 18, 19, 27 Powerstock/Zefa; p. 14 BSIP; p. 15 Tudor Photography; p. 16 Action Plus.
Cover photograph by Powerstock/Zefa.

Every effort has been made to contact copyright holders of any material reproduced in this book. Any omissions will be rectified in subsequent printings if notice is given to the publisher.

Some words are shown in bold, **like this.** You can find out what they mean by looking in the glossary.

CONTENTS

WHAT DOES MY SKIN DO?

Skin is an all-over protection suit. It separates and protects the inside of your body from the world outside. It keeps dirt, germs, and other harmful things, such as the Sun's rays, from getting into the body. It also stops moisture that is inside the body from getting out. The insides of your body are very moist and, without skin, they would quickly dry out.

Germs

Germs are **bacteria** and **viruses** that attack parts of your body and make you ill. Some germs do get inside your body when you eat and drink and breathe in air. The rest of your body, however, is protected by skin. If you cut or scrape your skin, you have to clean the wound and cover it to keep out dirt and germs.

This girl's skin is covered in mud. The mud will not harm her because her skin will keep any dirt or germs from getting inside her body.

Burns

You can see how important skin is by looking at what happens when some of it is lost by being burnt or scalded. Burns are caused by some chemicals and by electricity as well as by flames. Very hot liquid and steam scalds the skin. If you touch something that is too hot, you will get a mild but painful burn. Small, light burns heal themselves, but large or deep burns must be treated in the hospital. Serious burns destroy the skin. This makes it easy for germs to get inside the body. The burns must be treated quickly, so the body does not dry out.

Skin is waterproof. It stops water from leaking into and out of your body.

WHY DOES MY SKIN FLAKE?

If your skin becomes very dry, it becomes flaky. Skin is made up of two layers, the **dermis** and the **epidermis.** Both layers consist of millions of tiny **cells,** but the cells in the outer layer, the epidermis, are all dead. These dead cells are tough and hard to protect you against knocks and scrapes. As they gradually flake off they are replaced by new cells from the dermis below. Dead cells flake off all the time but they are usually so small you are not aware of them. In fact, most of the dust in your home consists of flakes of dead skin.

This photo shows what the surface of the skin looks like through a microscope. You can see the flakes of dead skin.

Inside the skin

Skin consists of much more than skin cells. It contains **glands** that produce sweat or oil, and the roots of your hair and your nails. Tiny tubes of blood thread their way through the skin, bringing food and oxygen to all the living cells. **Nerve endings** tell your brain what your skin is feeling.

Hair

Long, thick hair grows from your scalp, the skin that covers your head. Fine hairs cover most of the rest of your skin, except the palms of your hands and the soles of your feet. An oil gland just below the epidermis makes oil that keeps each hair soft and flexible.

A TYPICAL SQUARE CENTIMETER OF SKIN CONTAINS:

- 15 hairs
- 15 oil glands
- 100 sweat glands
- 21 inches (55 centimeters) of nerves
- 500,000 dead and dying cells.

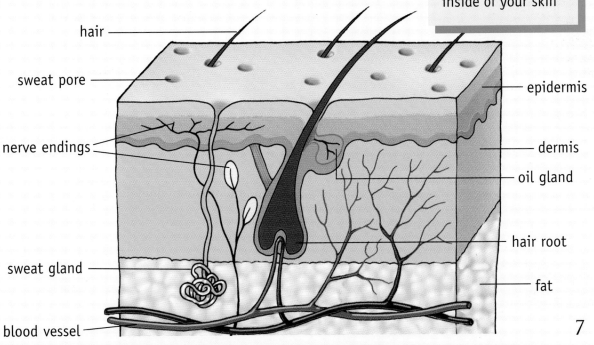

A magnified drawing of the inside of your skin

hair

sweat pore

nerve endings

sweat gland

blood vessel

epidermis

dermis

oil gland

hair root

fat

HOW THICK-SKINNED AM I?

Your skin varies in thickness on different parts of your body. The thickest skin is on the soles of your feet, where it is about 5 millimeters thick. If you walk around in bare feet a lot, the **epidermis** will become even thicker. The epidermis contains a special substance called **keratin** that makes the outer skin cells hard and tough.

Thin skin

Your skin is thinnest on your eyelids. Here it is only 1–2 millimeters thick. It is so thin that you can see a change from light to dark with your eyes closed.

Gravel hurts your feet, but some people have such a thick layer of skin on their feet that they can walk over gravel and rocks without feeling any pain.

Hard pads

If you do something that continually rubs part of your skin, the epidermis will become thicker there. If you like swinging from monkey bars, for example, thick pads of hard skin called calluses will form on the palms of your hands, just below your fingers.

Blisters

A blister protects your skin when it is rubbed away too quickly for the skin below to replace the lost **cells.** For example, you may get blisters if you go on a long walk and your shoes rub the back of your heels. The shoes rub away the top layer of skin so that the delicate layer of living skin below is unprotected. A blister contains liquid that cushions the skin below.

The skin on parts of this boy's palms has grown thicker from being rubbed on the monkey bars.

WHY DO I GET SUNBURN?

The Sun's rays contain harmful **radiation** that can damage **cells** in the body. Skin protects the body from radiation but it can get burned in the process.

Too much sun

The skin can only take a certain amount of radiation. If it is exposed to too much sun, it becomes red and sore. If the burn is mild, the redness fades in a few hours. But if it is severe, the skin may become swollen and peel off before the burn fades. Too much sunshine can also make you feel sick, weak, and dizzy. You may even get a fever.

This man did not use enough sunscreen. He has a sunburn. His red skin will feel hot and sore later.

Strongest sunshine

The Sun's rays are strongest when they are most directly overhead. This means that they are strongest in the summer and from the late morning until the middle of the afternoon. But the Sun's rays can still harm you at other times of the day and year. The Sun's rays are stronger the nearer you are to the equator, an imaginary line drawn around the center of the Earth, halfway between the North and South Poles.

Protecting yourself from the Sun

The best way to protect your skin from the Sun is to keep it covered. You should protect your back and chest by always wearing a shirt or T-shirt. Protect your head with a hat, and protect your eyes with sunglasses. Rub any bare skin with sunscreen. The Sun's rays travel through clouds and through water, so you must still protect your skin on cloudy days and when you are swimming.

Sunscreen protects your skin from the sun. Remember to rub in more lotion every hour or two, and after you go swimming.

Melanin

The body has its own defense against the Sun's rays. Inside your skin are **cells** that produce **melanin,** a substance that absorbs the **radiation.** As the Sun shines on your skin, it makes more melanin. This makes your skin darker because melanin is the substance that gives it its color. The more melanin you have in your skin, the better protected you are from the sun.

Special cells in the skin called melanocytes produce melanin. The melanin spreads throughout the **epidermis.**

Skin color

Some people are born with more melanin in their skin than others. The color of human skin varies from black through all shades of brown to yellow, pink, and white. You inherit your skin color from your parents and, the more melanin you have, the darker your skin will be.

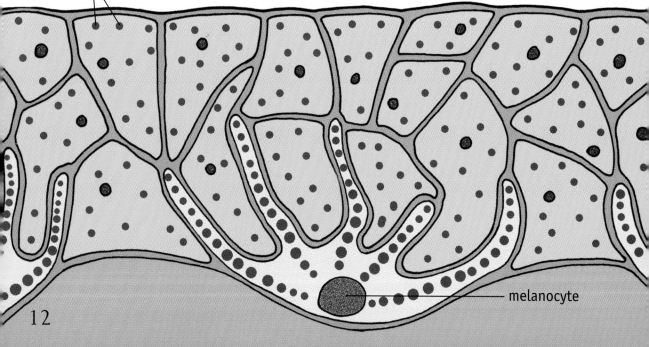

grains of melanin in epidermis

melanocyte

Safe tanning

The Sun's rays are so damaging that you cannot rely only on your natural melanin. Some people with red hair and fair skin burn very easily. Without sunscreen, light-skinned people should spend no more than 15 minutes a day in the Sun at first, and increase the time slowly, by 10 to 15 minutes a day. Using sunscreen allows you to stay in the Sun longer than your skin's natural protection allows. Remember to apply the cream before you go into the Sun and reapply it every few hours.

People have different colors of skin, depending on whether they have a lot of melanin or only a little.

SUN PROTECTION

The sun protection factor (SPF) on your sunscreen bottle tells you how long you can stay in the Sun.
- SPF 2   twice as long as normal
- SPF 6   six times as long as normal
- SPF 12   12 times as long as normal

WHAT ARE FRECKLES?

Freckles are small spots of darker skin, usually on the face, and sometimes on the arms and hands. The number of freckles increases during the summer, when they also become darker. Freckles form where there is more **melanin** in the skin.

Melanocytes

The cells that produce melanin are called melanocytes. Everyone has roughly the same number of them but some people's melanocytes produce more melanin than other people's. People with white and fair skin have melanocytes that produce very little melanin. People with black or darker skin have melanocytes that produce lots of melanin. Freckles are small patches of skin that have extra melanin.

This boy has freckles across his nose and over his cheeks. They increase in the summer and fade in the winter.

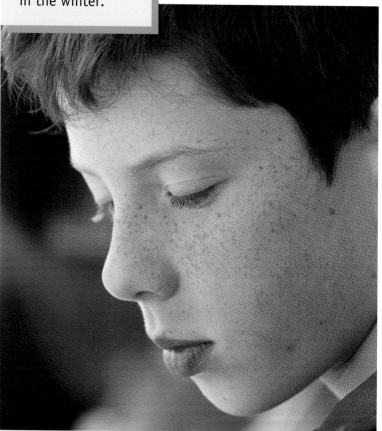

Moles

A mole is a patch of dark skin. It may be raised or flat, and is caused by cells that contain melanin. Some moles may be present at birth but most appear while you are a child. Moles tend to run in families and are very common: most adults have about 40 moles. Moles are usually harmless. Sometimes a mole may become unhealthy. If you have a mole that hurts, bleeds, or changes suddenly, then you should see a doctor. You may need to have the mole removed.

Birthmarks

Birthmarks are patches of skin that may be raised or flat, and are present from birth. They are made by large **blood vessels** close to the surface of the skin. Lighter birthmarks usually disappear on their own. Dark ones can be made lighter by being treated with laser beams.

This person has several moles on his arm. Moles stay the same all year.

WHY DO I GET RED WHEN I AM TOO HOT?

You often turn red when you have been running or exercising. Muscles make heat, and the heat is taken around the body by your blood. When you are hot, the tiny **blood vessels** in the skin become wider. This allows more blood to come to the surface of the body where it cools down. The extra blood makes your skin look red.

This girl's face is red and hot. Extra blood is being pumped into her skin, where it can cool down faster.

Sweating

When you are hot, sweat **glands** in the skin pump out extra sweat. Salty water then covers your skin and helps to cool you down. As it dries, it takes heat from your body and turns this into water vapor. Every part of your skin contains sweat glands. They lose moisture all the time, but you usually do not notice. Some parts of the body, such as the armpits, contain more sweat glands than other parts. As sweat **evaporates,** it leaves behind salt and a substance called urea. You need to bathe regularly so that these salts do not clog the skin or make you smelly.

Heat control

Part of the brain, called the hypothalamus, keeps your body temperature from getting too high or too low. When the temperature of your blood changes, it takes action. When the blood is too hot, it sends signals to the sweat glands and the blood vessels in the skin.

SWEAT

The body produces from one to two pints (up to one liter) of sweat a day. The palms of the hands, soles of the feet, and the forehead produce the most sweat.

Tennis players and other athletes make so much sweat their shirts become soaked.

WHAT CAUSES GOOSE BUMPS?

When you are cold the hairs on your skin stand up. They do this to trap air close to your skin to help to keep you warm. Each hair has a tiny muscle in the skin that tenses to pull the hair up. Goose bumps are the hard bumps made by these tiny, tense muscles. This is like a bird fluffing its feathers to trap air when it is cold.

Shivering

When you are cold, your body shivers. The muscles work together to make you tremble. As your lower jaw shivers, your teeth close and unclose rapidly, making a chattering sound. Muscles make heat as they work, so shivering helps to warm you up.

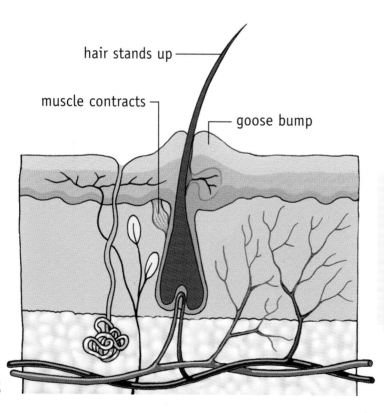

hair stands up

muscle contracts

goose bump

Goose bumps help warm you up when you are cold by making the fine hairs on your skin stand up.

18

Pale skin

Your body also acts to stop heat from escaping from it. Most heat is lost through your skin so the tiny **blood vessels** in your skin become narrower. This means that less blood comes into the skin and your skin looks much paler. If your feet or hands become very cold, they may become numb so that they cannot feel things properly. This is because the blood vessels have become so narrow that very little blood is reaching them. Stamping your feet and rubbing your hands will help to bring more blood to them.

Keeping warm

When the temperature of your blood drops, goose bumps, shivering, and the blood vessels in your skin all work together to make you warmer. Putting on warmer clothes and having a warm drink will also help warm you up when you are cold.

When the weather is very cold you must dress warmly. Make sure that your head, feet, and hands are well protected from the cold and the snow.

WHY DOES HAIR GROW THICKEST ON MY HEAD?

Hair keeps your head warm and plays an important part in how you look. Whether you braid your hair or have it loose, and whether you have bangs or not changes your appearance.

The long hairs that grow from your scalp help to keep you and your head warm. The body can lose a lot of heat through the scalp and hair acts like an animal's fur to keep heat in. This is important because the brain, below the scalp, needs to be warm to work well.

How hair grows

Hair is made of dead **cells.** It contains a strong substance called **keratin.** This is the same substance that makes your nails hard and the outer layer of skin tough. New hair cells form in the root of the hair, in a pocket in the skin called a **follicle.** As new cells are made, the older cells above them are pushed up through the skin to form the hair that you see. The hairs on your head grow about ¼ inch (1 cm) every month.

Each individual hair grows for about six years before it drops out.

Baldness

After a hair has dropped out, the hair root rests for about three or four months and then starts to grow a new hair. Some men become bald as, one by one, their hair roots stop producing new hairs. Baldness tends to run in families.

COUNTING HAIRS

You have from 100,000 to 120,000 hair follicles on your scalp. Every day 30 to 60 of your hairs fall out.

This photo shows what a hair looks like under a microscope. Each hair is built up of layers of cells.

WHY DO PEOPLE HAVE DIFFERENT COLORED HAIR?

Black is the most common hair color, but hair can be brown, or different shades of red, blonde, gray, or white. **Melanin** gives your hair its color. The more melanin your body makes, the darker your hair will be. People with blonde or fair hair have very little melanin. Those with red or brown hair have some melanin but not as much as people with black hair.

These children have different colored hair. You inherit your natural hair color from your parents.

Changing the color of hair

Some people change the color of their hair by dyeing it or bleaching it. Hair dye gives hair a different color, while bleaching removes the natural color. As people grow old their hair may change color naturally. The hair loses its color and becomes gray or white.

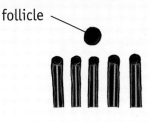

follicle

follicle

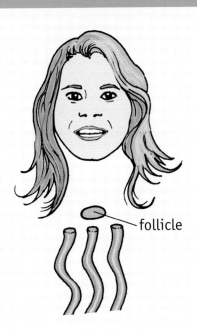

follicle

follicle

Straight or curly?

Whether your hair is straight, wavy, or curly depends on the shape of the **follicles** that the hairs grow from. Straight hair grows from round follicles, while wavy and curly hair grow from oval and from flat follicles. The flatter the follicle, the curlier the hair. Some people use chemicals to change their hair. Straight hair can be permed to make it curlier, and curly hair can be straightened.

Looking after your hair

You need to wash your hair regularly to keep it clean. You also need to cut off the ends from time to time, even if you are growing your hair. The end of a hair is the oldest part of it, and after a while it begins to split. Trimming off the ends stops them from splitting.

How straight or curly your hair is depends on the shape of the hair follicles in your scalp.

WHY DOESN'T IT HURT WHEN I CUT MY NAILS?

Cutting your nails does not hurt because there are no nerves in the nails. Like your hair, your nails are made of dead **cells** and contain **keratin.** This is the substance that makes them tough and hard. Nails are flat, horn-like plates that protect the ends of your fingers and toes. They give your fingertip something to press against to help you pick up very small items, such as pins or grains of rice.

How nails grow

New nail cells are made in the **nail bed** in the skin. As new cells are made, the older cells above them are pushed up through the skin.

A nail grows from special cells in the nail bed near the ends of the fingers and toes.

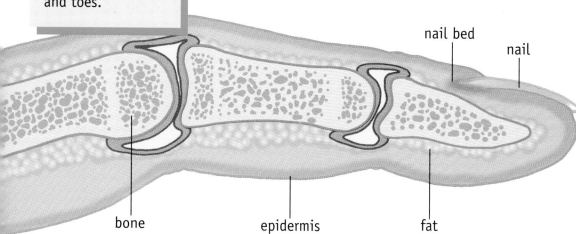

nail bed

nail

bone

epidermis

fat

24

Nails are white but look pink where the **epidermis** is so thin that the **blood vessels** below show through. Cutting the white tip of the nail does not hurt, but if the pink part of the nail breaks the skin below hurts.

Cutting your nails

Keeping your nails cut short stops dirt from getting trapped under them. Fingernails are usually cut or filed to a smooth, round shape, but it is better to cut toenails straight across. This helps to prevent a painful, ingrown toenail, caused when the nail grows into the flesh at the side of the nail.

It is a good idea to keep your nails smooth and short so that they do not break easily. Use nail clippers or an emery board. Do not bite your nails.

HOW FAST DO NAILS GROW?

Fingernails grow faster than toenails. Fingernails grow about 1 $\frac{1}{4}$ (3.5 cm) a year. Most people's nails break before they grow very long.

WHICH PART OF MY SKIN IS MOST SENSITIVE?

Different parts of the body are sensitive to different things. For example, bathwater feels hotter to your feet than it does to your hand. If you wanted to feel how rough or smooth something is, you would feel it with your fingertips, not the back of your hand. If someone pinches you on the back, it will not feel as painful as if they pinched your arm.

Skin contains nerve endings that tell you how hot or cold something is and what it feels like.

Nerves in the skin

You feel things in your skin because it contains different kinds of **nerve endings.** One kind of nerve ending reacts to heat, while another kind reacts to cold. Three different kinds react to light touch, heavy pressure, and pain. An area of skin that has a lot of one particular kind of nerve ending is sensitive to that thing.

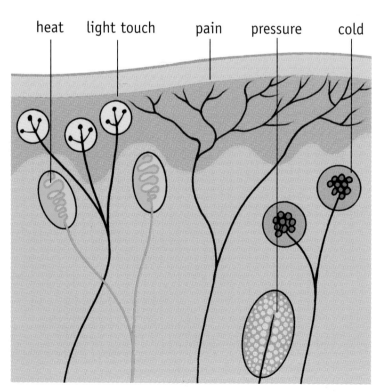

heat   light touch   pain   pressure   cold

Fingertips

Your fingertips are particularly sensitive to light touch. You use your fingers to pick up small objects, to write, and to tap the keys of a phone or computer. People with large hands and big fingers are usually better at doing things such as threading a needle or fastening small buttons, than people with thin fingers. The ridged pattern of skin on the tips of the fingers makes them even more sensitive. If this ridged skin is damaged, the fingertips are much less sensitive.

FINGERTIPS

No two people have the same pattern of ridges, so no one has the same fingerprints as you. Even identical twins have different fingerprints.

People who cannot see can read books printed in braille. In braille, each letter is shown by a pattern of dots that the person feels with her fingertips.

Lips and tongue

Your lips and tongue are packed with each kind of **nerve ending.** This makes them especially sensitive to hot and cold food and to touch and pain. If you bite your tongue by mistake, you will know how painful it is. And, when a tooth falls out, the gap left behind feels enormous to your tongue, but does not appear so large when you check in a mirror.

Pain

Pain protects your skin from harm. If you felt no pain, you would not realize when your skin and flesh was being burned, cut, or damaged. All parts of the body except the hair and nails contain nerve endings that react to pain. They tell you when there is something wrong. For example, your throat hurts when you are sick, and it hurts to move your hand when your wrist is broken.

This boy carefully sips a cup of hot chocolate. He uses his lips to tell how hot it is, so that he does not burn his mouth.

BODY MAP

The skin

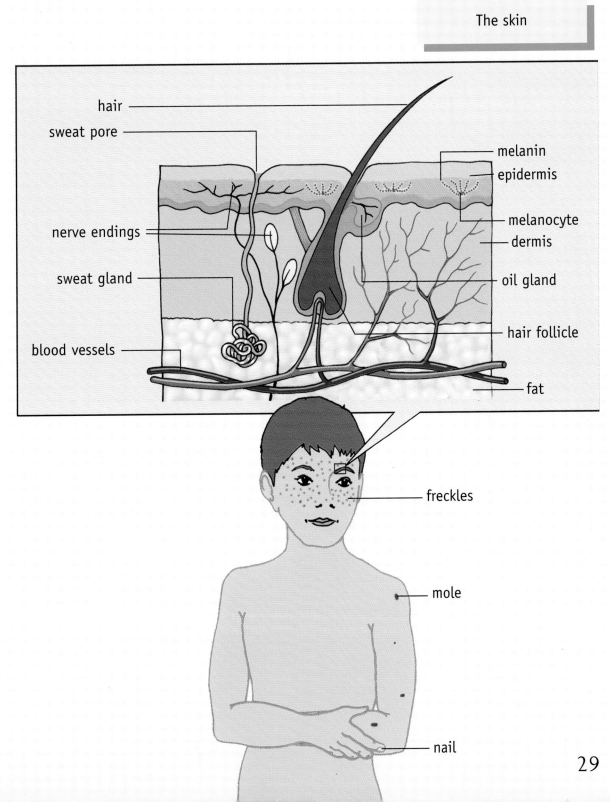

- hair
- sweat pore
- melanin
- epidermis
- nerve endings
- melanocyte
- dermis
- sweat gland
- oil gland
- blood vessels
- hair follicle
- fat
- freckles
- mole
- nail

GLOSSARY

bacteria   tiny living things. Some kinds of bacteria are germs that cause disease.

blood vessels   tubes through which blood moves around the body

cells   smallest building blocks of living things. The body has many kinds of cells, including skin cells, blood cells, and hair cells.

dermis   layer of skin beneath the epidermis

epidermis   tough, outer layer of skin

evaporate   to turn from liquid, for example water, into gas or vapor

follicle   small pocket in the skin from which a hair grows

germ   bacteria or virus that makes you ill

glands   parts of the body that produce particular substances, such as sweat and saliva

keratin   chemical substance that makes skin, nails, and hair strong and hard

melanin   chemical produced by the body and responsible for skin, hair, and eye color

nail bed   part of the skin from which a nail grows

nerve ending these receive messages that tell the brain what the skin feels

radiation rays of energy from the Sun

virus kind of germ that is even smaller than bacteria

FURTHER READING

Goode, Katherine. *Skin and Hair*. Farmington Hills, Mich.: Blackbirch Press, 2000.

Gordon, Sharon. *Sunburn*. Danbury, Conn.: Children's Press, 2002.

Rourke, Arlene. *Skin*. Vero Beach, Fla.: Rourke Publications, 1987.

INDEX